# GOD IS...

THE NAMES OF GOD

# KEN HEMPHILL

LifeWay Press® • Nashville, Tennessee

© 2017 LifeWay Press®

ISBN: 9781462747764
Item: 005794291

Dewey Decimal Classification: 231
Subject Headings: GOD—ATTRIBUTES \ NAMES \ PERSONAL NAMES

**Eric Geiger**
*Vice President, LifeWay Resources*

**Gena Rogers**
**Brian Gass**
*Content Editors*

**Michael Kelley**
*Director, Groups Ministry*

Send questions/comments to: Content Editor, *Bible Studies for Life: Adults*, One LifeWay Plaza, Nashville, TN 37234-0175; or make comments on the Web at BibleStudiesforLife.com.

Printed in the United States of America.

For ordering or inquiries, visit lifeway.com; write LifeWay Small Groups; One LifeWay Plaza; Nashville, TN 37234-0152; or call toll free (800) 458-2772.

We believe that the Bible has God for its author; salvation for its end; and truth, without any mixture of error, for its matter and that all Scripture is totally true and trustworthy. To review LifeWay's doctrinal guideline, please visit lifeway.com/doctrinalguideline.

All Scripture quotations, unless otherwise indicated, are taken from the the Christian Standard Bible®. Copyright 2017 by Holman Bible Publishers. Used by permission.

*Bible Studies for Life: Adults* often lists websites that may be helpful to our readers. Our staff verifies each site's usefulness and appropriateness prior to publication. However, website content changes quickly so we encourage you to approach all websites with caution. Make sure sites are still appropriate before sharing them with students, friends, and family.

# contents

# Social Media

Connect with a community of *Bible Studies for Life* users. Post responses to questions, share teaching ideas, and link to great blog content. **facebook.com/biblestudiesforlife**

Get instant updates about new articles, giveaways, and more. **@BibleMeetsLife**

# The App

*Bible Studies for Life* is also available as an eBook. The eBook can be opened and read with the *Bible Studies for Life App*, a free app from the iOS App Store or the Google Play Store.

# Blog

At **biblestudiesforlife.com/blog** you will find additional resources for your study experience, including music downloads provided by LifeWay Worship. Plus, leaders and group members alike will benefit from the blog posts written for people in every life stage—singles, parents, boomers, and senior adults—as well as media clips, connections between our study topics, current events, and much more.

# Training

For helps on how to use Bible Studies for Life, tips on how to better lead groups, or additional ideas for leading this session, visit: **ministrygrid.com/web/biblestudiesforlife.**

## *"God" is not His only name.*

You are probably known by different names. Those names reflect both your character and your relationships with those around you. For example, people who know me professionally call me Dr. Hemphill, yet others who know me personally call me Ken. My children call me Daddy and my grandkids call me Papa.

Not surprisingly, God has also been known by many names throughout the centuries.

The many names of God revealed in Scripture tell us much about His character. Those names invite us to know Him in a growing, intimate relationship. Knowing these names is important for three reasons:

▶ **God's name is inherently great.** "Lord, our Lord, how magnificent is your name throughout the earth!" (Ps. 8:1). Understanding the names of God will enable us to praise and worship Him more effectively.

▶ **God's name protects and benefits us.** "The name of the Lord is a strong tower" (Prov. 18:10). God's various names can be a tremendous aid to effective and specific prayer.

▶ **We represent God's name and must bring honor to it.** God gave Ten Commandments, and one of those Commandments has to do with His name: "Do not misuse the name of the Lord your God" (Ex. 20: 7). This command means far more than avoiding its use in vulgar or slang expressions. It means the people of God must reflect His name or character in their lives.

The names of God are a love gift to us. God reveals Himself *fully* so that we might experience His *fullness*. As we look at six of those names, we'll discover truths about the lovely character of our God.

## *Ken Hemphill*

Ken is husband to Paula, father to three daughters, and grandfather to ten grandchildren. He is a pastor who is passionate about the church and God's Word. He has served in many capacities in Southern Baptist life and is a prolific author. He is currently the Director for Church Planting and Revitalization at North Greenville University. Ken has authored numerous books, including *The Names of God*.

# 1 | OUR PROVIDER

*What's one of the hardest things you've been asked to do?*

*QUESTION #1*

*Trust God to meet our needs.*

# THE BIBLE MEETS LIFE

We've all made decisions to take on a daunting task, but it can be especially difficult when someone else makes that decision for you. The soldier who is "volunteered" for an assignment. The employee who is transferred to a new task or city. The student who is called on by the instructor to show the rest of the class how to solve "x." In those moments, our minds can be dominated by a single thought: *How am I going to do this?*

A few years ago, my wife, Paula, and I chose to move closer to our extended families. That might not seem like a hard decision, but things didn't fall together the way we expected. To make it even more challenging, my wife was diagnosed with cancer in the midst of the transition. We moved ahead, though, choosing to trust God and not our circumstances. We trusted and God provided.

When we look back, we can see God's hand at work. Our home has given us a quiet retreat—a wonderful healing place for Paula. God provides what we need, when we need it. Abraham knew this too. God truly is our Provider, and Abraham saw God's provision as he trusted Him during a great test of his faith.

# WHAT DOES THE BIBLE SAY?

## *Genesis 22:1-2*

**¹ After these things God tested Abraham and said to him, "Abraham!" "Here I am," he answered. ² "Take your son," he said, "your only son Isaac, whom you love, go to the land of Moriah, and offer him there as a burnt offering on one of the mountains I will tell you about."**

Abraham is commonly seen as a great example of someone who exercised strong faith. (See Heb. 11:8.) But Abraham's journey wasn't always easy. In fact, there were moments when he faltered:

▶ In his fear, Abraham claimed Sarah was not his wife—twice! (See Gen. 12:12-13; 20:1-3.)

▶ In his doubt, Abraham attempted to "help" fulfill God's promise through having a son by Sarah's slave Hagar. (See 18:1-3.)

In Genesis 22, Abraham faced his greatest test of faith. Verse 1 begins with an interesting phrase that is easy to overlook: "After these things." Moses, the writer of Genesis, wanted us to think back over Abraham's long journey that had led him from Ur of the Chaldeans to this very conversation with God.

God called to Abram when he was 75 years old (see Gen. 12:4), instructing him to leave his land, his relatives, and his father's house—everything that was familiar and comfortable. In return, God promised to bless Abram by making him into a great nation that would bless all the nations of the earth. (See v. 2.) This was problematic because Abraham had no children and his wife, Sarah, was barren. Even so, "Abram believed the LORD, and he credited it to him as righteousness " (15:6).

Abraham eventually did have a son, Isaac, although it took 25 years for God's promise to be fulfilled. (See 21:1-7.) Genesis 22 took place several years after Isaac's birth.

> *What's your initial reaction to these verses?*

*QUESTION #2*

Given Abraham's story, God's command in verse 2 is difficult to understand: "Take your son … your only son Isaac, whom you love, go to the land of Moriah, and offer him there as a burnt offering on one of the mountains I will tell you about."

Notice God's detailed description of Isaac: "your son … your only son Isaac, whom you love." This wasn't simply "a son" God required of Abraham. It was *his only son*. It was Isaac, the son *whom you love*. This son was not only dear to Abraham, he was essential to God's promises concerning the blessing of the nations—yet he was about to be offered as a sacrifice.

> **How do Abraham's actions in these verses demonstrate faith?**
>
> QUESTION #3

## Genesis 22:3-10

³ So Abraham got up early in the morning, saddled his donkey, and took with him two of his young men and his son Isaac. He split wood for a burnt offering and set out to go to the place God had told him about. ⁴ On the third day Abraham looked up and saw the place in the distance. ⁵ Then Abraham said to his young men, "Stay here with the donkey. The boy and I will go over there to worship; then we'll come back to you." ⁶ Abraham took the wood for the burnt offering and laid it on his son Isaac. In his hand he took the fire and the knife, and the two of them walked on together. ⁷ Then Isaac spoke to his father Abraham and said, "My father." And he replied, "Here I am, my son." Isaac said, "The fire and the wood are here, but where is the lamb for the burnt offering?" ⁸ Abraham answered, "God himself will provide the lamb for the burnt offering, my son." Then the two of them walked on together. ⁹ When they arrived at the place that God had told him about, Abraham built the altar there and arranged the wood. He bound his son Isaac and placed him on the altar on top of the wood. ¹⁰ Then Abraham reached out and took the knife to slaughter his son.

We can hear Abraham's faith in his instructions to the young men: "Stay here with the donkey. The boy and I will go over there to worship; then *we'll* come back to you" (emphasis added). How could he be so confident? The writer of Hebrews gave us insight into Abraham's thoughts as he took his son to Mount Moriah: "He considered God to be able even to raise someone from the dead; therefore, he received him back, figuratively speaking" (Heb. 11:19). Abraham was convinced that God, who had already performed one miracle by putting life into a barren womb, could raise Isaac from the dead. In short, Abraham had arrived at a point in his faith journey where he was confident he could trust God with his most valued possession: his only son.

The text gives us no clue as to how much time passed between verses 8 and 9. Having arrived at the place God designated, Abraham built the altar and arranged the wood in preparation for the sacrifice. This work might have taken considerable time, and I've often wondered if any additional dialogue passed between Abraham and Isaac. The text is silent. We are only told with utter simplicity that Abraham "bound his son Isaac and placed him on the altar on top of the wood," and then raised his knife to kill his beloved son.

Just reading the account leaves us nearly breathless. There's no doubt Abraham was committed to obey the command of God. Yet we should understand that Abraham's actions were based on his understanding of God's character. Our circumstances never test the faithfulness of God; they only test our understanding of His character and purpose.

> **When have you experienced a time of testing?**

**QUESTION #4**

## Genesis 22:11-14

**¹¹ But the angel of the LORD called to him from heaven and said, "Abraham, Abraham!" He replied, "Here I am." ¹² Then he said, "Do not lay a hand on the boy or do anything to him. For now I know that you fear God, since you have not withheld your only son from me." ¹³ Abraham looked up and saw a ram caught in the thicket by its horns. So Abraham went and took the ram and offered it as a burnt offering in place of his son. ¹⁴ And Abraham named that place The LORD Will Provide, so today it is said: "It will be provided on the LORD's mountain."**

This place of divine encounter became sacred for Abraham, and so he called it "The LORD Will Provide." This is the literal translation of the name *Jehovah Jireh*. The Hebrew word *jireh* can be translated "to see." We may wonder what the connection is between "seeing" and "providing." We can make the connection with the English noun "provision," a compound made up of two Latin words which when taken together mean "to see beforehand." God's pre-vision leads to His provision. God knew before Abraham ever reached Moriah that he would need a sacrifice; therefore, God personally provided the ram.

This is an amazing picture of salvation. Before the foundation of the world, God had prior vision of man's sin and rebellion. Seeing our need, He made provision for our redemption by providing a lamb of sacrifice—Jesus, "his one and only Son" (John 3:16).

Notice that it was Abraham's obedience that unleashed God's blessings in his life. (See Gen. 22:16-18.) For us as well, obedience is the key to growing faith. James spoke to this issue with great clarity when he compared those who hear God's Word and refuse to act with those who hear and do act. The latter will be blessed in what they do. (See Jas. 1:23-25.)

If you desire to unleash God's blessing in your life—if you want to discover that God is your Provider—then obey His Word. Obey immediately and without reservation, and see all that God will provide.

> *How can our actions and attitudes demonstrate that we serve the God who provides?*

*QUESTION #5*

# OUR PROVIDER

**Physically:**

1     2     3     4     5     6     7     8     9     10

(Not very trusting)                                    (Very trusting)

**Emotionally/Relationally:**

1     2     3     4     5     6     7     8     9     10

(Not very trusting)                                    (Very trusting)

**Spiritually:**

1     2     3     4     5     6     7     8     9     10

(Not very trusting)                                    (Very trusting)

What are some specific ways you recognize that God has provided for you recently?

"If God sends us on strong paths,
we are provided strong shoes."

—CORRIE TEN BOOM

# LIVE IT OUT

God will use challenging circumstances to lead us to a deeper understanding of His ability to provide for our needs. How will you apply these truths this week? Consider these suggestions:

▶ **Identify your Isaac.** What circumstance, person, or thing are you having the most difficulty placing in God's care? Pray this week for the faith necessary to let go.

▶ **Place your Isaac on the altar.** Abraham had to first gather the resources necessary to make a sacrifice before he could find God's provision. Identify concrete steps you can take to place your "Isaac" in God's care.

▶ **Look for God's provision.** Write down the ways God provides for you this week. Make known to others the good things God is providing in your life.

You can experience a breakthrough in your faith walk when you are willing to trust God with those things you hold most precious. Make that decision today and trust *Jehovah Jireh,* the God Who Provides.

My *thoughts*

# 2 | OUR HEALER

*When have you admired a renovation project?*

*QUESTION #1*

*God is the only one who can restore us and make us whole.*

# THE BIBLE MEETS LIFE

Works of art like Leonardo da Vinci's *Mona Lisa* and *The Last Supper* are universally recognized as great masterpieces, but most people don't realize the images we admire are quite different from what da Vinci first painted. *Mona Lisa* has darkened over time because of the varnishes used on it. Original fine details are now obscured. *The Last Supper* has deteriorated due to mildew. Early on, well-meaning painters attempted to clean it and repaint sections. In the process, they covered up da Vinci's actual work. Restoration is needed when we want to return to the artist's original design.

When left to themselves, objects like art, houses, and old cars lose their luster and even fall apart. And so do we. When left to ourselves, we drift from God's original plan and design for our lives. We take our eyes off Him. We often complain about Him while forgetting all He has done for us.

In short, we need restoration and healing.

In the Book of Exodus, the Israelites lost their focus, yet God showed Himself to be the God who restores. He is the Lord, our Healer.

# WHAT DOES THE BIBLE SAY?

## Exodus 14:29-31

**[29] But the Israelites had walked through the sea on dry ground, with the waters like a wall to them on their right and their left. [30] That day the LORD saved Israel from the power of the Egyptians, and Israel saw the Egyptians dead on the seashore. [31] When Israel saw the great power that the LORD used against the Egyptians, the people feared the LORD and believed in him and in his servant Moses.**

The parting of the Red Sea was an incredible miracle that sealed God's rescue of His people from their slavery in Egypt. Not surprisingly, that event holds a prime position as a symbol of God's salvation in the Old Testament. Isaiah later wrote: "Wasn't it you who dried up the sea, the waters of the great deep, who made the sea-bed into a road for the redeemed to pass over? And the redeemed of the LORD will return and come to Zion with singing, crowned with unending joy. Joy and gladness will overtake them, and sorrow and sighing will flee" (Isa. 51:10-11).

The Israelites had seen a clear demonstration of God's great power. As a result, "the people feared the LORD and believed in him and in his servant Moses." When they reached the other shore, the Israelites sang a song of celebration praising God for His deliverance. (See Ex. 15:1-18.) The song not only celebrated their present victory over Pharaoh; it also looked forward to their victorious conquest and settlement of the promised land. As we'll see, however, those songs didn't last very long. In fact, the Israelites' rejoicing turned quickly to grumbling when they were confronted with the reality of their freedom from Egypt.

What was true of the Israelites is often true of us today. Indeed, we often find that a testing of our faith will follow moments of spiritual victory. The question is whether we can still sing of God's glorious holiness even when we face moments of spiritual drought.

> *What have you learned about God from firsthand experience?*
>
> **QUESTION #2**

## Exodus 15:22-24

**22 Then Moses led Israel on from the Red Sea, and they went out to the Wilderness of Shur. They journeyed for three days in the wilderness without finding water. 23 They came to Marah, but they could not drink the water at Marah because it was bitter—that is why it was named Marah. 24 The people grumbled to Moses, "What are we going to drink?"**

Only a few days into the journey, the people of Israel began to grumble and complain, frustrated by the lack of water. When the Israelites saw Marah in the distance, they thought it was an oasis and likely believed their problems were solved. But their hope was dashed to pieces when they discovered the wells contained "bitter" (non-potable) water. Many artesian wells are bitter and unpleasant because of mineral salts. This one was not simply unpleasant; it may have been dangerous to their health.

The Israelites responded the way we typically do when things don't go our way: they complained. They demanded of Moses, "What are we going to drink?" How quickly a hero can become a scapegoat!

While their grumbling was aimed explicitly at Moses, it was implicitly directed at God, who had appointed Moses as their leader. Moses made this connection clear when Israel grumbled later about the lack of food: "He has heard the complaints that you are raising against him. Who are we? Your complaints are not against us but against the LORD" (Ex. 16:8). Sadly, God's people are described as complaining over twelve times during their wilderness wanderings.

> *How does complaining impact our connection with God?*
>
> **QUESTION #3**

The apostle Paul used the grumbling nature of the Israelites to warn believers in Corinth about such behavior, along with craving evil things, idolatry, immorality, and more. (See 1 Cor. 10:6-11.) We tend to treat grumbling, griping, and complaining as minor issues, hardly worthy of mention since "everyone does it." Yet Paul treated grumbling as a major offense and insisted it must be avoided.

The Israelites' thirst caused them to forget the deliverance they had recently enjoyed by the power of God. The contrast is striking between the faith they expressed in praise after crossing the Red Sea and the lack of faith when they encountered a challenge just three days into their journey. The matter was one of perspective. Could Israel trust God to work in every circumstance based on His character?

It's possible to grumble inwardly without verbalizing it. When we allow struggles and doubts to cause us to blame God for our circumstances, we're falling into the same pattern of behavior as the Israelites did in the wilderness. When we allow anxiety to rule our lives, we're focusing on circumstances rather than God's provision.

## Exodus 15:25-27

**25 So he cried out to the LORD, and the LORD showed him a tree. When he threw it into the water, the water became drinkable. The LORD made a statute and ordinance for them at Marah, and he tested them there. 26 He said, "If you will carefully obey the LORD your God, do what is right in his sight, pay attention to his commands, and keep all his statutes, I will not inflict any illnesses on you that I inflicted on the Egyptians. For I am the LORD who heals you." 27 Then they came to Elim, where there were twelve springs and seventy date palms, and they camped there by the water.**

God once again provided for the Israelites in a miraculous way, showing that He's not only powerful to deliver His people, but can and will sustain them. In addition, God made "a statute and ordinance for them." This statute contained a condition, "If you will carefully obey," which was followed by a promise: "I will not inflict…." The Old Testament contains numerous examples of "if/then" covenants. They demonstrate that God's blessings flow through the obedience of His children.

> **What are some different ways God heals and restores His people?**

QUESTION #4

In this case, God's promise was related specifically to the illnesses that had been "inflicted on the Egyptians." Surely the Israelites would have connected God's turning of the Nile to blood (see Ex. 7:14-25) with the undrinkable water at Marah. If Israel would carefully obey the Lord, they would not find the water God provided to be bitter because He is "the LORD who heals you." This is the name *Jehovah Rapha*.

The word *Rapha* occurs about sixty times in the Old Testament; it always refers to restoring, healing, or curing. It's frequently used in relation to physical healing, but it also can relate to moral and spiritual healing. At Marah, Jehovah revealed Himself to be the only source of true wholeness. He alone has the power to change the bitter experiences of life into something sweet.

God mercifully sustained the people at Marah, but there's more to the story. God led them from Marah "to Elim, where there were twelve springs and seventy date palms, and they camped there by the water." The numbers seven and twelve (and multiples of those numbers) appear throughout Scripture representing completeness. Elim was a place of completeness—a refuge that pointed to the abundant and healing provision of *Jehovah Rapha*.

We should never overlook the most important way *Jehovah Rapha* heals: through Jesus Christ. "He himself bore our sins in his body on the tree; so that, having died to sins, we might live for righteousness. By his wounds you have been healed" (1 Pet. 2:24). God promises healing for your deepest pains, your disappointments, your past, and your sins. He can turn your bitterness into sweet refreshment. If you've been sidetracked at Marah, bitter in soul and spirit, the only way to travel from Marah to Elim is to turn to *Jehovah Rapha*. Jesus is our *Jehovah Rapha*—our God who heals!

> *How can our actions and attitudes demonstrate that we follow the God who heals and restores?*
>
> **QUESTION #5**

# GOD OUR HEALER

*Healing and restoration can look very different in each believer's life. Use the space below to illustrate what God's restoration has looked like in your life. You may sketch a picture, write a poem, or use words and symbols to tell your story.*

**What did you learn about God our Healer through these experiences?**

"Heal me, LORD, and I will be healed; save me, and I will be saved, for you are my praise."

—JEREMIAH 17:14

# LIVE IT OUT

How should we respond when we find ourselves drinking from the bitter wells of Marah? Consider taking one of these steps this week:

▶ **Listen.** Listen earnestly to the voice of God. What is He trying to teach you in your present circumstances? What have you learned about God from these events? Change your perspective by seeing what God is doing on your behalf.

▶ **Obey.** Look to see if there are areas of disobedience in your life. Repent and turn from any disobedient actions or attitudes. Turn to the One who desires to heal you. Obedience flows from an accurate understanding of God's character.

▶ **Encourage.** Encourage someone you know who is drinking from bitter waters. Point them to Christ who offers healing, hope, and abundance.

You may not feel like a work of art right now, but the Bible assures each and every one of us that we've been created in God's image. If you want to move away from a place of bitterness, turn to *Jehovah Rapha,* the God Who Heals.

My *thoughts*

# 3 | OUR BANNER

**What are some things we rely on for protection?**

*QUESTION #1*

*We are always covered by God's protection.*

# THE BIBLE MEETS LIFE

The United States flag represents a lot of things to its citizens: freedom, democracy, justice, and home. Seeing the flag unfurled inspires a feeling of patriotism in many of us. For so many who served in the military or who lost a family member in war, the flag reminds them of courage and sacrifice.

For American citizens abroad needing assistance, the American flag also represents protection. When an American citizen steps onto the grounds of the U.S. embassy, the stars and stripes remind them they are now under the protection of the United States.

We face times when life throws us such a curve that we can feel alone and exposed—even when we're surrounded by others. In those moments, we feel vulnerable and under attack. In one moment of Israel's history, they too were vulnerable and under attack. But God Himself showed that He was on their side; He was their Banner, standing over them with His sovereign protection. We are not alone. We stand under another flag, a banner of protection: God Himself. He stands over every issue we face. God covers us with His protection.

# WHAT DOES THE BIBLE SAY?

## *Exodus 17:8-10*

**8 At Rephidim, Amalek came and fought against Israel. 9 Moses said to Joshua, "Select some men for us and go fight against Amalek. Tomorrow I will stand on the hilltop with God's staff in my hand." 10 Joshua did as Moses had told him, and fought against Amalek, while Moses, Aaron, and Hur went up to the top of the hill.**

The Israelites were now camped at Rephidim, and again the people had no water to drink. (See Ex. 17:1.) Unfortunately, the people responded in their usual way: they grumbled. Although they were testing God, the Lord provided water by instructing Moses to strike the rock with his staff. As when the people had complained about an earlier water problem (see Ex. 15:22-27), God miraculously provided this time too.

The Israelites were about to face a new—and perhaps greater—challenge to their faith. Thirst was the least of their worries because the Amalekites confronted them at Rephidim. The Israelites and the Amalekites had been enemies for generations. The Amalekites were the descendants of Amalek, a grandson of Esau. (See Gen. 36:12.) Even though they were direct descendants of Isaac, they became enemies of Israel, a constant threat to their spiritual and national life. Forty years after the events in Exodus 17, Moses still described the Amalekites as people who "did not fear God" (Deut. 25:18).

It was obvious how the Amalekites' viewed God because they attacked His people all along the way after they left Egypt. Clearly, however, God was with the Israelites. He had performed miracle after miracle in His work of delivering the people from slavery. God's hand was on the Israelites, but the Amalekites didn't care. They still attacked.

Thankfully, we are not left on our own in our struggles and battles. As we will see in the next few verses, the Israelites were not alone—and neither are we.

> *What daily challenges can make us feel like we're in a battle?*

**QUESTION #2**

## Exodus 17:11-13

**¹¹ While Moses held up his hand, Israel prevailed, but whenever he put his hand down, Amalek prevailed. ¹² When Moses's hands grew heavy, they took a stone and put it under him, and he sat down on it. Then Aaron and Hur supported his hands, one on one side and one on the other so that his hands remained steady until the sun went down. ¹³ So Joshua defeated Amalek and his army with the sword.**

The battle plan to defeat the Amalekites may seem a bit unorthodox but it was certainly effective. Moses commissioned Joshua to select men to join him in battle as they confronted the enemy. While Joshua was leading the troops, Moses, Aaron, and Hur stood on the top of a nearby hill. Moses had God's staff in his hand.

Nothing indicates any fear or confusion, which might have been expected, among the Israelites as they faced Amalek. These were wandering people, ill-equipped for battle, yet as long as Moses held up the staff Israel prevailed. But when his arms grew tired and he let his hand down, Amalek had the upper hand. Ultimately, Aaron and Hur supported Moses' hands "so that his hands remained steady until the sun went down." As a result, "Joshua defeated Amalek and his army with the sword."

What made the difference? It was not simply Moses' visible presence and dramatic posture on the hilltop with his hand in the air that inspired confidence in his troops; it was that he was holding up God's staff. Though this staff was likely nothing more than a shepherd's staff, God used it as an object lesson to show all Israel His power to accomplish His work.

This staff became a visible sign that God was with Moses. This simple staff became the staff of God that Moses used to bring various plagues, part the Red Sea (see 14:15-16), and strike the rock to provide water for the thirsty Israelites. (See 17:5-6.)

> *How can we maintain our reliance on God's power when the battle is long?*
>
> **QUESTION #3**

# GOD OUR BANNER

*Use the space below to draw a banner that represents how you feel about God. Include your favorite Bible verse, attributes of God, or significant milestones in your walk with Him.*

*Write a prayer of praise to the Lord acknowledging His work of protection in your life.*

"The safest place in all the world is in the will of God, and the safest protection in all the world is the name of God."

—WARREN WIERSBE

The staff in Moses' hand was an ordinary implement any shepherd would carry. It had nothing magical about it and no inherent power in it. It was simply a sign of God's presence and power to accomplish His work among His people. Israel prevailed in battle when Moses' hand lifted up the presence of God for all to see. We also prevail in our spiritual battles when God's presence and power are in our lives. It is critical to note that, before we put on the spiritual armor (see Eph. 6:10-18), we are given clear instruction about the source of our strength. "Finally, be strengthened by the Lord and by His vast strength" (v. 10).

We must never underestimate the craft and cunning of our spiritual adversary nor overestimate our own strength. We cannot win spiritual battles in our own strength. We can walk in victory over sin only when we stand under God's banner of protection and put on the spiritual armor He has provided.

## Exodus 17:14-16

**14 The Lord then said to Moses, "Write this down on a scroll as a reminder and recite it to Joshua: I will completely blot out the memory of Amalek under heaven." 15 And Moses built an altar and named it, "The Lord Is My Banner." 16 He said, "Indeed, my hand is lifted up toward the Lord's throne. The Lord will be at war with Amalek from generation to generation."**

*What does God's banner of protection look like in your life?*

*QUESTION #4*

After the victory, God's first command was for Moses to write and recite to Joshua His declaration: "I will completely blot out the memory of Amalek under heaven." The Israelites would have other encounters with the Amalekites, whose atrocities were such that God later commanded King Saul to completely annihilate them. Unfortunately, Saul was disobedient. (See 1 Sam. 15:2-9.) The Amalekites were not completely defeated until the eighth century BC, in the days of Hezekiah. (See 1 Chron. 4:41-43.)

In response to God's work, Moses built an altar and called it "The LORD Is My Banner." God had shown Israel yet another aspect of His character. Israel had already discovered that God was their healer (*Jehovah Rapha*). Now they understood He was also their banner of protection—their *Jehovah Nissi*.

The staff or banner in Moses' hand was a visible image of the protection and the power of God, who provided the victory over Amalek. The Israelites were to understand that their victory was because God was a banner over them. He was their protection.

One of the most famous banners in the Old Testament also appeared while the Israelites were in the wilderness. Once again, the people grumbled about the lack of bread and water. "Then the LORD sent poisonous snakes among the people, and they bit" many of them so that they died (Num. 21:5-6). They confessed to Moses their sin against the Lord, and he interceded for them before God.

"Then the LORD said to Moses, 'Make a snake image and mount it on a pole. When anyone who is bitten looks at it, he will recover.' So Moses made a bronze snake and mounted it on a pole" (Num. 21:8-9).

Jesus referred to the banner in His conversation with Nicodemus about the need to be born again to enter the Kingdom of God. Jesus told him, "Just as Moses lifted up the snake in the wilderness, so the Son of Man must be lifted up, so that everyone who believes in him may have eternal life" (John 3:14-15).

Jesus is "Our Banner" who provides forgiveness of sin and eternal life. He "covers" us with His protection and victory.

> *How can our actions and attitudes demonstrate that we serve the God who protects?*

*QUESTION #5*

# LIVE IT OUT

How will the truth that Jesus is "Our Banner" make a difference in your life? Consider these suggestions:

▶ **Trust.** Have you accepted Jesus as your banner of forgiveness? If not, commit your life to Him and trust Him for salvation.

▶ **Pray.** Specifically pray for individuals this week to experience the presence and protection of Christ in their lives. Pray also that these people would be keenly aware Christ is the One who goes with them.

▶ **Be bold.** If you're facing a difficult relationship or assignment from God, step out in trust because Christ goes with you. Rest confidently in His presence and protection.

As awesome as it is to look up to the flag of the great country in which you live, there is something even better when you trust in Christ. You can live a victorious Christian life as you stand under *Jehovah Nissi,* God Our Banner.

*My thoughts*

# 4 | OUR PEACE

*Where do you go when you need some peace and quiet?*

QUESTION #1

*God's peace helps us rise above our circumstances.*

# THE BIBLE MEETS LIFE

I grew up in a time when "peace" was a popular slogan, but it was also an excuse for a way of life that was often anything but peaceful. It's hard to imagine anyone who wouldn't want peace, but the daily news feeds make us painfully aware that peace is severely lacking: wars and skirmishes around the world; riots on college campuses; and political unrest in our communities. We long for authentic peace.

Peace is not simply something needed "out there." We need peace in our churches, our homes, and our own hearts. Wouldn't it be wonderful if we could live with an absence of conflict in our lives, a time with no squabbling or obstacles? Even when we experience moments of "peace and quiet," they are often short-lived.

Peace is possible, and it is a peace that is far more than just an absence of conflict. The Old Testament judge Gideon lived in a time of conflict, but he discovered a peace in the midst of his circumstances. He discovered he could trust God to give peace because He is our Peace.

# WHAT DOES THE BIBLE SAY?

## *Judges 6:11-13*

**<sup>11</sup> The angel of the LORD came, and he sat under the oak that was in Ophrah, which belonged to Joash, the Abiezrite. His son Gideon was threshing wheat in the winepress in order to hide it from the Midianites. <sup>12</sup> Then the angel of the LORD appeared to him and said: "The LORD is with you, valiant warrior." <sup>13</sup> Gideon said to him, "Please, my lord, if the LORD is with us, why has all this happened? And where are all his wonders that our fathers told us about? They said, 'Hasn't the LORD brought us out of Egypt?' But now the LORD has abandoned us and handed us over to Midian."**

It's one thing to be in the same room with people, but it's quite another for the people in that room to enjoy peace and unity. That was the case with the tribes of Israel. In the Book of Judges, the Israelites had entered the promised land, and the land had been divided among the tribes of Israel. But even though Israel occupied the land, no longer were the people united in heart and mind. They had lost the sense of being a unique people; they had compromised God's standards. The closing verse of the Book of Judges well summarizes this period: "Everyone did whatever seemed right to him" (21:25).

The Book of Judges is marked by a cyclical pattern: sin and rebellion, followed by punishment, then followed by a season of repentance and deliverance. The deliverer was usually an anointed "judge"—a leader provided by the sovereign hand of God. The judge would bring deliverance and spiritual renewal would come to the people for a season. Then the cycle of sin and punishment would be repeated. Ultimately, Israel lost the fruit of their land and labor.

Here the Israelites were again in the sinful phase of this cycle, so God disciplined them by allowing the Midianites to oppress them. The Israelites called out to God in their despair and the Lord sent a prophet.

> *Where do you see people questioning God's goodness and presence today?*

*QUESTION #2*

God in His mercy was prepared to send a deliverer. Without fanfare, we are told that the angel of the LORD sat under an oak tree as Gideon was beating out wheat in his winepress. This surely was an odd place to thresh wheat, but Gideon was hoping to hide from the Midianites. It seems even stranger that the angel called Gideon a "valiant warrior." After all, he was at that moment in a wine vat hiding from the enemy.

Gideon was focused on the difficult circumstances. He called into question the presence and power of God and asked why so many bad things were happening to Israel. His thinking was simple. If God was with them, the Midianites would not be pillaging their fields. The people of Israel would not be living like animals. He was correct in thinking God's people should not be living in defeat, but he was wrong to conclude their situation was due to the Lord's weakness.

Gideon's second question was similar to the first: "And where are all his wonders that our fathers told us about?" The Israelites frequently rehearsed the story of God's redemption and provision. They knew God had delivered Israel from bondage and miraculously saved them at the Red Sea and throughout the wilderness experience.

Like Gideon, when we focus on our circumstances we can't properly see God's hand at work. The result is a lack of peace and contentment.

## Judges 6:14-16

**14 The LORD turned to him and said, "Go in the strength you have and deliver Israel from the grasp of Midian. I am sending you!" 15 He said to him, "Please, Lord, how can I deliver Israel? Look, my family is the weakest in Manasseh, and I am the youngest in my father's family." 16 "But I will be with you," the LORD said to him. "You will strike Midian down as if it were one man."**

# GOD OUR PEACE

*Which of the following images reflect anxiety you've experienced in life?*

*How has God brought peace to you or others you know in some of these circumstances?*

"Thou hast taught me to say,
'It is well, it is well with my soul.'"

—HORATIO SPAFFORD

The Lord didn't directly answer Gideon's question or respond to his accusation that He had abandoned them. Instead, He gave Gideon a commission to "Go in the strength you have and deliver Israel from the grasp of Midian. I am sending you!"

But instead of responding in humble gratitude for the privilege God had given him, Gideon attempted a second strategic end run. This time he questioned his own ability. These responses sound much more pious and humble. "Please, Lord, how can I deliver Israel? Look, my family is the weakest in Manasseh, and I am the youngest in my father's family." While his protest may sound humble, it was simply an excuse and an affront to God. Gideon focused on his perceived shortcomings, but God had created Gideon and had specifically chosen him for this task.

God's response to Gideon was firm but reassuring. "But I will be with you." When God calls us to a task, He assures us of His presence and His power to enable us to accomplish our assigned mission. God accompanies us as we follow Him. This has been God's pattern and plan throughout time. The Great Commission is accompanied by the promise, "I am with you always, to the end of the age" (Matt. 28:20).

Gideon asked for a sign. He brought an offering and the angel touched it with the staff in his hand. As a result, fire sprang forth from the rock, consuming the offering. (See Judg. 6:17-21.) No doubt, the consuming fire leaping from a rock was a great clue for Gideon that he had received a message from God.

> *How do we recognize when God is calling us to a task?*
>
> **QUESTION #3**

## Judges 6:22-24

**22 When Gideon realized that he was the angel of the LORD, he said, "Oh no, Lord God! I have seen the angel of the LORD face to face!" 23 But the LORD said to him, "Peace to you. Don't be afraid, for you will not die." 24 So Gideon built an altar to the LORD there and called it The LORD Is Peace. It is still in Ophrah of the Abiezrites today.**

In the Old Testament, "the angel of the LORD" often referred to the presence of God Himself. So when the angel of the LORD disappeared right after causing Gideon's offering to be miraculously consumed by fire (see vv. 17-21), Gideon realized he had been in the presence of the LORD. His response was one of holy fear.

In that moment, Gideon realized he was in God's favor. Trouble was all around because of the Midianites, but God was with him—and that was all the assurance and peace he needed. In grateful response, Gideon built an altar and named it "The LORD Is Peace"—*Jehovah Shalom.*

> **How has God used our group to help you find peace in life?**
>
> QUESTION #4

The Hebrew word *shalom* is usually translated in English as "peace." *Shalom* is one of the most significant terms in the Old Testament. The fundamental idea conveyed by the word *shalom* is wholeness in one's relationship with God. It defines a harmony in the relationship based on completing a transaction. In our relationship with God it means a sense of contentment, freedom from guilt, and satisfaction with life itself. Of course, this does require that we must have a pure heart before God and live in obedience to His Word and His plan.

We might wonder how we, with our human failings, can ever be at peace with a holy God. We can only answer that question by understanding the full significance of the name *Jehovah Shalom.* The prophet Isaiah wrote that a child would be born who would be called Prince of Peace. (See Isa. 9:6.) The Prince of Peace died to reconcile sinful individuals to our holy God. Jesus is our peace; He tore down the wall that separates us from God and from others. (See Eph. 2:14.) Jesus is *Jehovah Shalom!*

> **How can our actions and attitudes demonstrate that we serve the God who is our peace?**
>
> QUESTION #5

# LIVE IT OUT

God's peace allows us to rise above our circumstances. How will you display that truth this week? Choose one of the following suggestions.

▶ **Receive Jesus as your Prince of Peace.** If you have never experienced God's peace, admit your sin, turn from it, and turn to Jesus by faith. Then you will live in peace with God.

▶ **Enjoy true *shalom* in your relationship with God.** If you have received Christ as Savior but are not experiencing wholeness, you may be stuck in a cycle of sin. Ask God to show you any areas of spiritual neglect and disobedience. Confess them, turn from them, and turn back to Him.

▶ **Live at peace with others.** Jesus our Peace has broken down all dividing walls. Is there a broken relationship in your life that needs to be made whole? Go to that person in the power of Christ and seek forgiveness and reconciliation.

The world rightly lifts up peace as a virtue. But the peace that comes from *Jehovah Shalom,* God Our Peace, is a peace that truly passes all human understanding.

My thoughts

# 5 | OUR SHEPHERD

When has a guide made an experience more memorable?

*QUESTION #1*

*God guides us as He walks with us.*

# THE BIBLE MEETS LIFE

Maps are good to direct you from one place to another, but you need to study them before leaving on a trip. If you don't know the route well, you will need to stop periodically and double-check the map.

GPS is better, but you still have to pay attention. You must glance continually at the screen to get a visual on how soon a turn is coming or listen intently to the verbal instructions.

The best way to travel is with someone who knows the route well. A guide can anticipate things and remind you to "get in the left lane" or "be prepared for a sharp turn." They often know shortcuts that the GPS is not clever enough to know. A guide can also provide "color commentary" as you travel, telling you interesting tidbits about places along the route.

Let's admit, we all need a guide to get through life. Even when we think we have things figured out, life inserts a roadblock and the journey changes. But God does for us just as a shepherd does for his flock. God is our Good Shepherd who guides us on the right path and in the right direction.

# WHAT DOES THE BIBLE SAY?

## Psalm 23:1-3

[1] **The LORD is my shepherd; I have what I need. [2] He lets me lie down in green pastures; he leads me beside quiet waters. [3] He renews my life; he leads me along the right paths for his name's sake.**

David very well may have written Psalm 23 during the latter years of his reign as Israel's king. It clearly has the ring of personal experience. It testifies to a faith tested by trials and a life mellowed and matured by the passing of years.

David had experienced conflict—both internal and external—including wars, family division, personal disappointments, discouragement, and despair. His hands were soiled by the murder of Uriah. His adulterous relationship with Bathsheba had ignited family fighting that led to ongoing conflict among family members. David experienced sin and the deep sorrow of its consequences; he knew the pain of one son's death and the rebellion of another who tried to take his kingdom.

Yet this psalm affirms that, through it all, David knew God as his tender Shepherd. The imagery in this psalm may go back to David's childhood experiences. As a shepherd boy, David was deemed an unlikely candidate to become the king of Israel. It is significant that David, the great warrior, was drawn to a simple but assuring depiction of God as a gentle Shepherd caring for the needs of His flock.

The profound impact of Psalm 23 is not discovering that God cares like a Shepherd, but the intimacy of the truth that God is *my* Shepherd. He is *the* Shepherd who "lets me lie down in green pastures"; who "leads me beside quiet waters." David knew he belonged to the Lord and that gave him calm assurance in the midst of trials.

> *In what ways have you experienced God's guidance in life?*
>
> **QUESTION #2**

David's expression of absolute trust was stated in profound simplicity: "I have what I need." He mentioned the green pastures and quiet waters first because they are fundamental needs of the sheep if they are to survive and grow. Sheep cannot continue to follow the shepherd without sufficient rest and adequate food. The shepherd must put himself at risk and often travel great distances to meet these basic needs, but he does so because his care and focus are on the sheep. Our satisfaction level is directly related to our proximity to the Good Shepherd.

The phrase "He renews my life" can convey two ideas. Renewal can refer to a straying sheep that has been brought back to the fold; it also may point to the deep renewal available to all sheep that remain in relationship with the shepherd. The two pictures are intertwined. God desires abundance for all His sheep, even the straying ones.

"He leads me along the right paths" simply means that we will be safe and productive because of the Shepherd's presence. This does not mean we will not face danger and difficulty as we follow the Shepherd. Verse 4 reminds us the sheep may travel through dark valleys, yet they can have courage in knowing they need not fear the danger as long as they remain near the shepherd.

The final phrase of verse 3—"for his name's sake"—serves as a refrain. The Good Shepherd would never lead His sheep in paths that would prove harmful or destructive because it is contrary to His character. God gives the guidance we need "for his name's sake."

## Psalm 23:4-5

**⁴ Even when I go through the darkest valley, I fear no danger, for you are with me; your rod and your staff— they comfort me. ⁵ You prepare a table before me in the presence of my enemies; you anoint my head with oil; my cup overflows.**

# GOD OUR SHEPHERD

1. A man who has served the Lord for many years now finds himself
   out of work through no fault of his own.

2. A teenager at your church has made a series of poor choices and is now
   in trouble with the authorities.

3. A couple in your neighborhood is considering moving to a new city
   to help with a church plant.

*How could God use you to work alongside Him as He leads
each of these individuals on their journey?*

"I am the good shepherd. The good shepherd
lays down his life for the sheep."

—JOHN 10:11

In verses 1-3, the shepherd is pictured as a guide who scouts the landscape to lead his flock to food, water, and rest. Now he is seen as coming alongside the sheep to personally escort the flock. When the sheep face the testing of a dark valley, he is by their side.

The rod and staff were the tools the shepherd used to protect and guide his sheep. The rod was a short, club-like stick worn on the belt and used against animals and thieves. The staff could serve as a walking stick, but when necessary, the shepherd employed it to keep the sheep from straying off the path.

When we feel the pressure of the staff, we might be tempted to react in anger. But we can trust our Shepherd is concerned for our care and protection. God's discipline is always motivated by His unchanging love. He guides us back onto the right path so that we will know His presence and experience His protection, even in the "darkest valley" (v. 4).

> **When have you experienced God's presence in a dark valley?**
>
> QUESTION #3

In verse 5, the imagery of the sheep and shepherd is exchanged for an even more intimate picture. David now pictured himself as a guest in the Lord's house.

Jesus the Good Shepherd reclined at a table with His disciples. Indeed, His last gathering with them before His crucifixion was when He kept the Passover with them. Jesus promised His disciples that He would one day eat and drink with them in His kingdom.

When we are walking through dark valleys of doubt, discouragement, and difficulty, how good it is to know God is and will be with us!

> **Which of the images in this passage is most meaningful to you right now?**
>
> QUESTION #4

## Psalm 23:6

**⁶ Only goodness and faithful love will pursue me all the days of my life, and I will dwell in the house of the LORD as long as I live.**

The promises of this psalm continue to heap one upon the other. We are not simply promised a celebratory meal which will soon be over. We are not simply guests; we are residents. We will live with God as long as we live—which is forever!

"Only goodness and faithful love will pursue me all the days of my life." "Faithful love" refers to God's covenant love promised to His own people. Throughout Scripture, we see the people of God continually relying on the bedrock truth that God is faithful; He exhibits His goodness and faithful love to His people.

David concluded that he would live in the presence of God with His unending goodness and faithful love "as long as I live." This phrase is literally "a length of days," which is not explicitly an expression for eternity. However, since God's covenant love has no end, the logic of the statement implies an eternal dwelling with God.

Jesus used the image of "the good shepherd" in John 10 to describe His own ministry. He contrasted the good shepherd to the stranger, the thief, the robber, and the hired hand. A thief and a robber desire only to steal and kill the sheep, and a hired hand flees when the sheep are threatened. In contrast, the Good Shepherd is willing to lay down His life for the sheep.

Jesus, God in human flesh, fully revealed what it means to address God as *Jehovah Rohi*. The Book of Revelation offers one final picture of Jesus, our Good Shepherd: "For the Lamb who is at the center of the throne will shepherd them; he will guide them to springs of the waters of life, and God will wipe away every tear from their eyes" (Rev. 7:17). The Good Shepherd is the Lamb of God who lays down His life for His sheep and the Lamb of God who is eternally our Good Shepherd.

> *How can our actions and attitudes demonstrate that we follow God as our Shepherd?*

**QUESTION #5**

# LIVE IT OUT

How will a relationship with the Good Shepherd make a difference in your life? Choose one of the following applications.

▶ **Rest and trust.** When God doesn't provide what you think you need, trust His goodness. Spend some time this week thanking Him for His protection.

▶ **Stay close.** Sin will keep you from experiencing all the good the Shepherd desires for you. Acknowledge and confess any sin that keeps you separated from the One who desires to lead you to still waters.

▶ **Slow down.** If you are rushed and harried, it may be that you aren't taking time for the Shepherd to feed you and restore your soul. Make changes to your schedule to ensure more quality time in God's Word.

We all need help with directions from time to time, whether we like to admit it or not. Thankfully we have the truest guide for life in *Jehovah Rohi,* God Our Shepherd.

My thoughts

# 6 | OUR RIGHTEOUSNESS

As a kid, what made you say "That's not fair!"?

QUESTION #1

*Because God is righteous, He will ultimately make all things right.*

# THE BIBLE MEETS LIFE

I have ten grandchildren, and I find myself repeating some of the same things my dad would say to me. For example, I'll sometimes hear one of them complaining about something that happened at school, and I'll hear: "That's just not fair!" In those moments, I echo what my father said to me: "Who said life would always be fair?"

I'm guessing you've heard that too. And if you're a parent, I'm guessing you've also said it.

Life isn't fair! It's frustrating when we see people with poor character and questionable morals seem to get ahead in life; meanwhile, those who seek to do right often fall behind. Such events might cause us to think that God is not fair. *Why doesn't He punish the unrighteous and reward the righteous?*

We are not the first ones to raise that question. God showed us much about Himself through the prophet Jeremiah. In Jeremiah 33, God revealed Himself as Our Righteousness; in so doing, He helps us deal with those "unfair" moments.

# WHAT DOES THE BIBLE SAY?

## *Jeremiah 33:3-5*

**3 Call to me and I will answer you and tell you great and incomprehensible things you do not know. 4 For this is what the Lord, the God of Israel, says concerning the houses of this city and the palaces of Judah's kings, the ones torn down for defense against the assault ramps and the sword: 5 The people coming to fight the Chaldeans will fill the houses with the corpses of their own men that I strike down in my wrath and rage. I have hidden my face from this city because of all their evil.**

Nearly a hundred years after Assyria had taken the ten northern tribes of Israel into captivity (see 2 Kings 17:6-18), Judah also stood on the brink of collapse. Jeremiah was God's spokesman during the latter part of these tumultuous years. His ministry began during the reign of the good king Josiah, who was profoundly moved when he rediscovered the Word of God. As a result, Josiah restored the temple and revived worship. (See 22:8-13; 23:4-25.) Unfortunately, the revival and reform which occurred during Josiah's reign ended abruptly after the young king's untimely death. (See 23:29-30.) Spiritual decline led to rapid moral decay and oppression; violence and political unrest were the order of the day.

We pick up the narrative over twelve years later, during the reign of King Zedekiah. King Nebuchadnezzar of Babylon was Judah's primary nemesis. Zedekiah sent two priests to Jeremiah asking the prophet to inquire to the Lord on their behalf. (See Jer. 21:2.) The prophet's response was an unexpected warning: God was going to use the Chaldeans to bring judgment upon His own people. (See vv. 4-7.) The Lord invited Judah to display the fruits of repentance and be restored (see 22:3-4), but Zedekiah and the people ignored the warning of the prophet and rejected the kindness of the Lord. Zedekiah imprisoned Jeremiah in the guards' courtyard, in an attempt to silence the prophet. Jeremiah told Zedekiah he would soon see Nebuchadnezzar face to face because he would be taken captive to Babylon. (See 32:1-5.)

*What captures your attention about God's character in these verses?*

QUESTION #2

The people of Judah must have wondered how to understand Jeremiah's message in light of God's promises and purposes for His own people. Had not God promised to establish David's throne forever? (See 2 Sam. 7:10-16.) Yet the people brought this on themselves through their own disobedience and sin!

God disciplines us just as He disciplined the people of Judah, but His purpose is to bring us back to Himself—and even into a closer walk with Him. God invites us to call to Him. We find the answers we seek and the hope we need when we call to Him. Then He reveals to us "great and incomprehensible things you do not know."

The "incomprehensible things" God would reveal remind us our knowledge is limited but God's knowledge is unlimited. God desires to answer the prayers of His people, but we must first cry out to Him.

Jeremiah had an even more dramatic word from God. God would raise up a Righteous Branch from the line of David, a King who would bring judgment and justice to the earth. He would be called "The LORD Is Our Righteousness" (Jer. 23:6)—*Yahweh Tsidkenu*.

## *Jeremiah 33:6-8*

**⁶ Yet I will certainly bring health and healing to it and will indeed heal them. I will let them experience the abundance of true peace. ⁷ I will restore the fortunes of Judah and of Israel and will rebuild them as in former times. ⁸ I will purify them from all the iniquity they have committed against me, and I will forgive all the iniquities they have committed against me, rebelling against me.**

The bad news is eclipsed by the good news that follows. God now would extend mercy to them—mercy that would result in health, healing, and an abundance of peace and truth. Both Judah and Israel would be brought back from captivity and reunited.

But the very best news of all was that God would deal with their sin. God Himself would bring health and healing, and the past sufferings of the people would be replaced by "the abundance of true peace." This unusual phrase suggests a lasting peace.

God also promised His people would return to their land and rebuild the nation as it was before the two kingdoms were divided. While God's judgment of sin is just, His mercy and kindness are abundant. His restoration of His people would be complete.

This good news culminates in the promise that God would deal with their sin problem. The Lord used three words to describe sin:

How have you experienced God's restoration?

QUESTION #3

▶ **Iniquity.** A word rooted in the idea of twisting or bending.

▶ **Iniquities.** A word that shares the same Hebrew root as the first, but it carries the idea of missing the mark.

▶ **Rebelling.** A term that means to resist authority or to rise in opposition against a ruler.

Despite the rebellion of God's people, His desire was to forgive and restore. The problem of our sin and rebellion is one that runs throughout the Bible, but alongside it is the testimony of God's desire to redeem and restore. The depravity of humanity is clear, but equally clear is God's solution. We want things to be just and right. We want life to go well—and so does God! Yet in those moments when it doesn't seem that life is either just or right, we should remember that God is at work!

## Jeremiah 33:14-16

¹⁴ **"Look, the days are coming"—this is the Lord's declaration— "when I will fulfill the good promise that I have spoken concerning the house of Israel and the house of Judah. ¹⁵ In those days and at that time I will cause a Righteous Branch to sprout up for David, and he will administer justice and righteousness in the land. ¹⁶ In those days Judah will be saved, and Jerusalem will dwell securely, and this is what she will be named: The Lord Is Our Righteousness."**

By announcing, "Look, the days are coming," Jeremiah declared the time was near at hand when the people would see the fulfillment of "the good promise" for both the house of Israel and the house of Judah. The promise concerned the restoration of the Davidic line. God would make things right!

Righteousness is not just a description—He is a Person! "The LORD Is Our Righteousness." God would "cause a Righteous Branch to sprout up for David," who would "administer justice and righteousness in the land." Of course, this "Righteous Branch" referred to the coming Messiah.

> *How do the promises in these verses point forward to Jesus?*
>
> QUESTION #4

The name of God that affirms His righteous character will also become the name of Jerusalem because the city will take on His character. Jerusalem would be restored and become what God always intended it to be—a city marked by righteousness. (See Isa. 1:26, 62:2-4; Jer. 3:17.)

Paul spoke of his own "righteous" accomplishments based on his strict adherence to the law. In Christ, he saw those accomplishments as mere rubbish. (See Phil. 3:4-7.) Why would this religious man consider his own righteousness as rubbish? "Because of him I have suffered the loss of all things and consider them as dung, so that I may gain Christ and be found in him, not having a righteousness of my own from the law, but one that is through faith in Christ—the righteousness from God based on faith" (vv. 8-9).

On those days where life doesn't go right, trust that God will ultimately make all things right. He will bring His righteousness to bear on all things, including the lives of those who follow Him.

> *How can our actions and attitudes demonstrate that we follow God who is Our Righteousness?*
>
> QUESTION #5

# GOD OUR RIGHTEOUSNESS

**R**-elationships that are pure and holy.

**I**-

**G**-

**H**-

**T**-

"Our righteousness is in Him, and our hope depends, not upon the exercise of grace in us, but upon the fullness of grace and love in Him, and upon His obedience unto death."

—JOHN NEWTON

# LIVE IT OUT

God is Our Righteousness. How will you let that truth make a difference in your life? Choose one of the following applications.

▶ **Confess.** Because God is righteous, He stands apart from sin. Enter into a relationship with Him, or restore your fellowship with Him, by confessing any sin in your life.

▶ **Trust.** Life is not always fair. Even when it feels like the wrong side is winning, God will have the final say. In the meantime, trust Him. He loves you, and in His righteousness, He will make things right.

▶ **Stand.** The trend in our culture is to believe we can each have our own definition of righteousness. Instead of becoming a standard to ourselves, Jesus is the standard for righteousness. Stand with Him and stand for Him in doing and proclaiming what is right.

We all have plenty of examples of life not being fair. Thankfully we know all will be made right in the end by *Jehovah Tsidkenu*, God Our Righteousness.

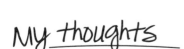

# MEANT

BY TONY EVANS

You've probably heard someone say something they probably shouldn't have said or done something that lacked tact, but someone else tried to cover it up with, "They meant well."

What they were saying is that even though what the person said or did created a negative reality, that was not their intention. Their motives were pure.

But that was not the case with Joseph's brothers when they stripped him of his coat and dumped him in a pit. Nor was that the case when they greedily plucked him from the pit and sold him for a profit to slave traders headed to a foreign land.

But God meant …

We read, "You planned evil against me; God planned it for good to bring about the present result—the survival of many people" (Gen. 50:20).

God's sovereignty does not only include good things, but it also includes the bad and what other people mean for harm.

Very few people get to God's intended purpose for their lives quickly. It takes time not only to develop you for your destiny but to develop your destiny for you. God is the master weaver, and things are rarely as they appear. That is why it is so critical to walk by faith and not by sight.

Have you ever seen an orchestra when musicians first come out and are getting ready to play? All of the instrumentalists are warming up at the same time, and it sounds like chaos. It sounds like no one on the platform even knows how to play. That is because all of the different sounds are discombobulated all over the place. There is no harmonizing taking place.

Then all of a sudden, out of nowhere it seems, a conductor walks out. He stands confidently and quietly in front of the musicians. He pulls out a small stick and raises it slightly. When he does, everyone in his or her chairs who had been playing their instruments sit up straight and look directly at him. Then when he taps the stick a couple of

times and begins to wave his hand, what had once appeared to be pure chaos now makes sense. The random, disconnected tunes that had previously polluted the air suddenly turn into a beautiful, powerful harmonious song.

Friend, if you feel like your life is in chaos, with so many disjointed and disconnected noises, don't leave the concert hall before the symphony swells. Don't check out on your faith. Wait for the Conductor to appear, because when the time is just perfect, He will bring harmony to discord. He will show up and turn a disappointment into a destiny.

> ## Detours begin to make sense when God brings life's ups and downs into harmony.

It may look like God has your life in bits and pieces right now. You can't possibly see how, or why, any of it could amount to much good. There doesn't appear to be a real connection to a lot going on. The delays are bitter. The disappointments leave a bad taste in your mouth. But when you allow God, in His providential care, to mix it all together according to His purposes and plan, all things will work together for our good. I promise. And the reason why I can promise is because God says so in His Word. It's probably a verse you have heard so many times that it may have somehow lost its impact, but if you will let the truth of it truly sink in, it can change your entire life.

"We know that all things work together for the good of those who love God, who are called according to his purpose" (Rom. 8:28). And that good will always be connected with conforming us to the image of Christ. (See v. 29.) For God is not just concerned about our circumstantial deliverance, but more importantly, He is concerned about our spiritual development. To that end, He will use all things to work together for good.

Even those things that others may have meant for evil.

All things means all things.

**Tony Evans** is founder and senior pastor of Oak Cliff Bible Fellowship in Dallas, founder and president of The Urban Alternative, former chaplain of the NFL's Dallas Cowboys, and present chaplain of the NBA's Dallas Mavericks. His radio broadcast, "The Alternative with Dr. Tony Evans," can be heard on nearly 1,000 U.S. radio outlets daily and in more than 130 countries. For more information, visit TonyEvans.org.

Excerpted from *Detours: The Unpredictable Path to Your Destiny* by Tony Evans. B&H Publishing Group © 2017.

## GENERAL INSTRUCTIONS

In order to make the most of this study and to ensure a richer group experience, it's recommended that all group participants read through the teaching and discussion content in full before each group meeting. As a leader, it is also a good idea for you to be familiar with this content and prepared to summarize it for your group members as you move through the material each week.

Each session of the Bible study is made up of three sections:

## 1. THE BIBLE MEETS LIFE.

An introduction to the theme of the session and its connection to everyday life, along with a brief overview of the primary Scripture text. This section also includes an icebreaker question or activity.

## 2. WHAT DOES THE BIBLE SAY?

This comprises the bulk of each session and includes the primary Scripture text along with explanations for key words and ideas within that text. This section also includes most of the content designed to produce and maintain discussion within the group.

## 3. LIVE IT OUT.

The final section focuses on application, using bulleted summary statements to answer the question, *So what?* As the leader, be prepared to challenge the group to apply what they learned during the discussion by transforming it into action throughout the week.

The *God Is …* leader guide contains several features and tools designed to help you lead participants through the material provided.

## QUESTION 1—ICEBREAKER

These opening questions and/or activities are designed to help participants transition into the study and begin engaging the primary themes to be discussed. Be sure everyone has a chance to speak, but maintain a low-pressure environment.

## DISCUSSION QUESTIONS

Each "What Does the Bible Say?" section features six questions designed to spark discussion and interaction within your group. These questions encourage critical thinking, so be sure to allow a period of silence for participants to process the question and form an answer.

The *God Is …* leader guide also contains follow-up questions and optional activities that may be helpful to your group, if time permits.

## DVD CONTENT

Each video features Ken Hemphill discussing the primary themes found in the session. We recommend you show this video in one of three places: 1) At the beginning of the group time, 2) After the icebreaker, or 3) After a quick review and/or summary of "What Does the Bible Say?" A video summary is included as well. You may choose to use this summary as background preparation to help you guide the group.

The leader guide contains additional questions to help unpack the video and transition into the discussion. For a digital leader guide with commentary, see the "Leader Tools" folder on the DVD-ROM in your Bible study kit.

For helps on how to use *Bible Studies for Life,* tips on how to better lead groups, or additional ideas for leading, visit: *ministrygrid.com/web/BibleStudiesforLife.*

## SESSION 1: OUR PROVIDER

*The Point:* Trust God to meet our needs.

*The Passage:* Genesis 22:1-14

*The Setting:* God called Abram (Abraham) to leave his homeland, with the promise that God would bring him to a new land and make from him a great nation. Despite God's promise, for many years Abraham's wife, Sarah, remained childless. Finally, at the age of 100, Abraham was able to see the fulfillment of God's promise when Sarah bore him a son they named Isaac.

QUESTION 1: What's one of the hardest things you've been asked to do?

> *Optional activity:* Distribute blank name tags and ask group members to fill out his or her tag with a fun nickname they've had. Ask for volunteers to share their nicknames and the meanings behind them. Use this activity to introduce the theme of this study which will look at six names of God and what they teach us about Him.

*Video Summary:* Session 1 opens our study of *God Is* by examining the Lord Our Provider—*Jehovah Jireh*—through the lens of Abraham's journey of faith. God had promised that Abraham would be the father of many nations. But just as we do, there were times when Abraham doubted God's provision. There are four specific steps in a journey of faith: (1) Faith always begins with the call of God. (2) Faith requires dependence on God. (3) Faith requires surrender. (4) Faith requires full reliance. Challenging circumstances are a platform for God to reveal more of Himself. We can always entrust into His care that which is most precious.

▶ WATCH THE DVD SEGMENT FOR SESSION 1. THEN USE THE FOLLOWING QUESTIONS AND DISCUSSION POINTS TO TRANSITION INTO THE STUDY.

- In what ways have you personally experienced God as your provider?
- When have you seen God use challenging circumstances in your life or the life of someone you know to reveal more of Himself?

## WHAT DOES THE BIBLE SAY?

▶ ASK FOR A VOLUNTEER TO READ ALOUD GENESIS 22:1-14.

Response: What's your initial reaction to these verses?

- What do you like about the text?
- What questions do you have about these verses?

▶ TURN THE GROUP'S ATTENTION TO GENESIS 22:1-2.

**QUESTION 2:** What's your initial reaction to these verses?

This question requires that group members interpret the biblical text as a way to move them toward identifying what this passage means and specifically what it means for them personally.

> *Optional follow-up:* What are the different ways Abraham could have responded to God's command?

**QUESTION 3:** How do Abraham's actions in these verses demonstrate faith?

This question first calls group members to define faith for themselves and second, identify how Abraham's actions in this passage demonstrate faith.

> *Optional follow-up:* What are some tactics we often use to delay or limit our obedience to God?

▶ MOVE TO GENESIS 22:3-10.

**QUESTION 4:** When have you experienced a time of testing?

This question is designed to give group members an opportunity to share from personal experience. Don't pressure them to share if they aren't comfortable. At the same time, don't discourage them from being vulnerable if they choose to do so.

> *Optional follow-up:* How did God provide for you during this time?

▶ CONTINUE WITH GENESIS 22:11-14.

**QUESTION 5:** How can our actions and attitudes demonstrate that we serve the God who provides?

Encourage group members to brainstorm specific ways they can live lives both individually and as a group that demonstrate they truly believe they serve a God who provides.

> *Optional activity:* Direct group members to complete the activity "Our Provider" on page 13 to show the myriad ways in which God has provided for each of us.

**Note:** The following question does not appear in the Bible study book. Use it in your group discussion as time allows.

**QUESTION 6:** How does Genesis 22:11-14 foreshadow the gospel?

Answering this question will require group members to interact with the biblical text. Guide them to discuss how God made provision for our redemption by providing a lamb of sacrifice.

## LIVE IT OUT

God will use challenging circumstances to lead us to a deeper understanding of His ability to provide for our needs. Encourage group members to consider these suggestions for applying this truth this week:

- **Identify your Isaac.** What circumstance, person, or thing are you having the most difficulty placing in God's care? Pray this week for the faith necessary to let go.

- **Place your Isaac on the altar.** Abraham had to first gather the resources necessary to make a sacrifice before he could find God's provision. Identify concrete steps you can take to place your "Isaac" in God's care.

- **Look for God's provision.** Write down the ways God provides for you this week. Make known to others the good things God is providing in your life.

*Challenge:* You can experience a breakthrough in your faith walk when you are willing to trust God with the things you hold most precious. Make a conscious decision to turn those things over to the Lord every day. Ask Him to make you aware of times when you aren't walking in faith and trusting Him to provide.

*Pray:* Ask for prayer requests and ask group members to pray for the different requests as intercessors. As the leader, conclude by thanking God for His awesome provision, especially the salvation provided for us in Jesus. Ask Him for courage for group members to share that truth with others this week.

## SESSION 2: OUR HEALER

*The Point:* God is the only one who can restore us and make us whole.

*The Passage:* Exodus 14:29-31; 15:22-27

*The Setting:* The Israelites had known nothing but slavery for centuries. But that changed when Yahweh, the one true God, sent His spokesman Moses to the Egyptian Pharaoh demanding that the Israelites be released from their captivity. As God displayed His might and mercy both in the Israelites' exodus from Egypt and their time of wandering in the wilderness, He called the Israelites into covenant relationship with Himself, a relationship demanding both trust in and obedience to Yahweh.

QUESTION 1: When have you admired a renovation project?

> *Optional activity:* Show a brief clip from one of your favorite home improvement shows. Ask: "What impresses you most about the host's ability to restore a house and create something new?"

> **Note:** Sample clips are available online. You can find a link at our blog: biblestudiesforlife.com/adultextra.

*Video Summary:* This week's video message looks at *Jehovah Rapha*—God Our Healer. In Exodus 15 we witness the Israelites grumbling. They are frustrated and looking for somewhere to place blame. When we grumble and complain, it's generally an indication that we're more focused on our circumstances than on our God. Only God can change the bitter experiences of our lives into sweet. Our God is a healing God.

▶ WATCH THE DVD SEGMENT FOR SESSION 2. THEN USE THE FOLLOWING QUESTIONS AND DISCUSSION POINTS TO TRANSITION INTO THE STUDY.

- Do you ever struggle with grumbling and bitterness? Explain.
- What does it mean to you that God is your healer?

## WHAT DOES THE BIBLE SAY?

▶ ASK FOR A VOLUNTEER TO READ ALOUD EXODUS 14:29-31; 15:22-27.

Response: What's your initial reaction to these verses?

- What questions do you have about these verses?
- What do you hope to learn this week about how God can restore you and make you whole?

▶ TURN THE GROUP'S ATTENTION TO EXODUS 14:29-31.

**QUESTION 2:** What have you learned about God from firsthand experience?

This question provides group members with an opportunity to share a personal story which also encourages the building of biblical community within the group.

> *Optional follow-up:* When have you seen God fight on your behalf?

▶  MOVE TO EXODUS 15:22-24.

**QUESTION 3:** How does complaining impact our connection with God?

To answer this question, group members will need to examine and identify times of complaining in their own lives that have impacted their connection with God. By identifying the effects complaining has had, they will be in a better position to avoid it in the future.

> *Optional follow-up:* When we complain, which characteristics of God are we calling into question?

▶  CONTINUE WITH EXODUS 15:25-27.

**QUESTION 4:** What are some different ways God heals and restores His people?

This question gives group members an opportunity to share ways they have experienced God's healing and restoration, as well as what they have observed in the lives of others. Encourage them to be specific.

> *Optional follow-up:* How have you experienced God's healing and restoration?

**QUESTION 5:** How can our actions and attitudes demonstrate that we follow the God who heals and restores?

This is a question that should be engaged and answered both by your group as a whole and individually by each group member. It will provide them with an opportunity to identify practical steps for positive action and prepare them to move on to discuss Question 6.

> *Optional activity:* Direct group members to complete the activity "God Our Healer" on page 21 to illustrate ways God has brought healing and restoration to their lives.

**Note:** The following question does not appear in the Bible study book. Use it in your group discussion as time allows.

**QUESTION 6:** In what ways can your life communicate to others that you believe and serve a God who heals and restores?

Try to steer group members away from taking theory; encourage them to get practical and specific.

## LIVE IT OUT

How should we respond when we find ourselves drinking from the bitter wells of Marah? Invite group members to consider taking one of these steps this week:

- **Listen.** Listen earnestly to the voice of God. What is He trying to teach you in your present circumstances? What have you learned about God from these events? Change your perspective by seeing what God is doing on your behalf.

- **Obey.** Look to see if there are areas of disobedience in your life. Repent and turn from any disobedient actions or attitudes. Turn to the One who desires to heal you. Obedience flows from an accurate understanding of God's character.

- **Encourage.** Encourage someone you know who is drinking from bitter waters. Point him or her to Christ who offers healing, hope, and abundance.

*Challenge:* You may not feel like a work of art right now, but the Bible assures each and every one of us that we've been created in God's image. Make a commitment to ask God every morning to help you see yourself as someone He has restored and made whole. Accept His healing, hope, and abundance.

*Pray:* Ask for prayer requests and ask group members to pray for the different requests as intercessors. As the leader, conclude by asking God to restore areas of your life that need healing or repair. Thank Him for allowing you the privilege of helping others find healing also.

## SESSION 3: OUR BANNER

*The Point:* We are always covered by God's protection.

*The Passage:* Exodus 17:8-16

*The Setting:* Moving on from Elim, the Israelites journeyed to the Wilderness of Sin, where they again fell into grumbling against God's spokesman, Moses, and his brother, Aaron. In their hunger, they complained that Moses and Aaron had led them out into the wilderness to die of starvation; they also longed for their former life in Egypt where there was plenty to eat. God mercifully provided the Israelites manna to eat. (See Ex. 16.) They then traveled on to Rephidim, where they again grumbled against Moses and complained of a lack of water. (See 17:1-3.) But in spite of the people's insults and testing of the Lord, God again graciously provided for their needs. (See vv. 4-7.)

QUESTION 1: What are some things we rely on for protection?

> *Optional activity:* To introduce the idea of protection, secure three or more of the following items: a lock, a blanket, a life jacket, a surge protector, or something else that communicates protection or security. Display these to your group and ask: "What do these things have in common?" Allow time for discussion. Explain that when used properly, these items provide protection.

*Video Summary:* The session 3 video message examines *Jehovah Nissi*—the Lord Our Banner. The story picks up in Exodus 17 where we find the Israelites still grumbling and complaining and preparing to go to battle with the Amalekites. God wanted them to trust Him daily for their provision. In this passage, the banner was a symbol of God's presence among His people. We have no power to win any spiritual battle in our own strength. Jesus Christ is our banner of protection.

▶ WATCH THE DVD SEGMENT FOR SESSION 3. THEN USE THE FOLLOWING QUESTIONS AND DISCUSSION POINTS TO TRANSITION INTO THE STUDY.

- When you find yourself in a storm, where do you first look for shelter? Be honest.
- Read Ephesians 6:10-18. Which piece of armor do you feel you need most right now? Explain.

## WHAT DOES THE BIBLE SAY?

▶ ASK FOR A VOLUNTEER TO READ ALOUD EXODUS 17:8-16.

Response: What's your initial reaction to these verses?

- What questions do you have about these verses?
- What new application do you hope to get from this passage?

▶ TURN THE GROUP'S ATTENTION TO EXODUS 17:8-10.

QUESTION 2: What daily challenges can make us feel like we're in a battle?

Direct group members to consider examples from their daily lives as well as stories they have heard through the media. This question will help them consider challenges that can distract us from living as those who are under God's protection.

> *Optional follow-up:* What's your typical reaction when you feel under attack?

▶ MOVE TO EXODUS 17:11-13.

QUESTION 3: How can we maintain our reliance on God's power when the battle is long?

This is an application question included to encourage group members to create steps they will take to act on the biblical principles presented in this session.

> *Optional activity:* Direct group members to complete the activity "God Our Banner" on page 27. As time permits, encourage volunteers to share their responses.

▶ CONTINUE WITH EXODUS 17:14-16.

QUESTION 4: What does God's banner of protection look like in your life?

Sharing and storytelling represent great ways for growing as a group. This question creates an environment for sharing relative to the text.

> *Optional follow-up:* How can we help one another in the battles we face?

QUESTION 5: How can our actions and attitudes demonstrate that we serve the God who protects?

The goal for this question is to help group members think through practical ideas for how they can live out what they truly believe about who God is. Encourage them to be specific in their responses and to push beyond the most obvious answers.

> *Optional follow-up:* In this week's text, the staff or banner in Moses' hand was a visible image of the protection and power of God. What other visible images of His protection can we find in Scripture?

**Note:** The following question does not appear in the Bible study book. Use it in your group discussion as time allows.

QUESTION 6: Refer back at Exodus 17:11-13. Who plays the roles of Aaron and Hur in your life?

This question requires group members to closely examine the Scripture passage in order to make personal application.

## LIVE IT OUT

How will the truth that Jesus is "Our Banner" make a difference in your life? Encourage group members to consider these suggestions:

- **Trust.** Have you accepted Jesus as your banner of forgiveness? If not, commit your life to Him and trust Him for salvation.

- **Pray.** Specifically pray for individuals this week to experience the presence and protection of Christ in their lives. Pray also that these people would be keenly aware that Christ is the One who goes with them.

- **Be bold.** If you're facing a difficult relationship or assignment from God, step out in trust because Christ goes with you. Rest confidently in His presence and protection.

*Challenge:* As awesome as it is to look up to the flag of the great country in which you live, there is something even better when you trust in Christ. You can live a victorious Christian life as you stand under *Jehovah Nissi*, God Our Banner. In what area of your life will you step out in trust this week?

*Pray:* Ask for prayer requests and ask group members to pray for the different requests as intercessors. As the leader, conclude by thanking God once again for His awesome protection. Ask Him for courage to share this aspect of His character with others in the coming week.

*The Point:* God's peace helps us rise above our circumstances.

*The Passage:* Judges 6:11-16,22-24

*The Setting:* Once the Israelites were settled in the promised land, they forsook the Lord and worshiped other gods. God punished them by handing them over to their enemies. When the Israelites cried out to God, He would raise up an individual to deliver the people. Unfortunately, the Israelites never seemed to learn and time and again returned to their false gods. On one occasion, God handed the Israelites over to the Midianites for seven years, after which the Israelites cried out to the Lord for deliverance. (See Judg. 6:1-10.)

QUESTION 1: Where do you go when you need some peace and quiet?

> *Optional activity:* In advance, locate a one-minute portion of a video clip of ocean waves with soothing music. Prepare to share the video clip using your laptop or tablet. Instruct volunteers to spend one minute without thinking of any of the stress or cares they may have at this time; ask them to imagine themselves alone on a beautiful beach, with nothing to do and nothing to worry about. Challenge group members to enjoy a time of peace before asking Question 1.

*Video Summary:* The week's video message looks at *Jehovah Shalom*—God Our Peace. In our text we see that the promised land has been inhabited but there's still no unity or peace. We all long for an absence of conflict in our lives. Even when we have those moments of "peace and quiet," they are often short-lived. But God offers us a far greater and lasting peace, even while facing conflict with others or battling our circumstances. In Gideon's encounter with God, he discovered he could trust God to give the Israelites peace because of who God is.

▶ WATCH THE DVD SEGMENT FOR SESSION 4. THEN USE THE FOLLOWING QUESTIONS AND DISCUSSION POINTS TO TRANSITION INTO THE STUDY.

- In what areas of your life are you needing God to bring peace?
- In what areas are you already experiencing true peace?

## WHAT DOES THE BIBLE SAY?

▶ ASK FOR A VOLUNTEER TO READ ALOUD JUDGES 6:11-16,22-24.

Response: What's your initial reaction to these verses?

- What do you like about the text?
- What new application do you hope to receive about God's peace?

▶ TURN THE GROUP'S ATTENTION TO JUDGES 6:11-13.

**QUESTION 2:** Where do you see people questioning God's goodness and presence today?

This question is designed to help group members consider instances they encounter in their day-to-day lives when others question God's goodness and presence. Answers will vary based on individual experiences.

> ***Optional follow-up:*** What do you find surprising about these initial verses?

▶ MOVE TO JUDGES 6:14-16.

**QUESTION 3:** How do we recognize when God is calling us to a task?

This question invites members of the group to share personal testimonies of ways they have been able to apply the scriptural text to their daily lives. If they can't think of a personal example, encourage them to share a time they observed this in the life of someone they know.

> ***Optional activity:*** Direct group members to complete the activity "God Our Peace" on page 35. As time permits, encourage volunteers to share their responses.

▶ CONTINUE WITH JUDGES 6:22-24.

**QUESTION 4:** How has God used our group to help you find peace in life?

This question provides another opportunity for group members to share from personal experience while also illustrating the power and importance of being a part of a biblical community.

> ***Optional follow-up:*** What are some ways God has helped you find peace in life?

**QUESTION 5:** How can our actions and attitudes demonstrate that we serve the God who is our peace?

Use this question as an opportunity to remind group members that you aren't looking for a specific answer for most discussion questions. You're asking for their personal thoughts and ideas.

**Note:** The following question does not appear in the Bible study book. Use it in your group discussion as time allows.

**QUESTION 6:** When have you questioned your suitability for a God-given task?

Refer back to Judges 6:14-16. This question will allow group members an opportunity to share from personal experience as well as acknowledge and reflect on what they truly believe about who God is and what He can do.

> ***Optional follow-up:*** What made you question your suitability for the task?

## LIVE IT OUT

God's peace allows us to rise above our circumstances. How will you display that truth this week? Invite group members to choose one of the following suggestions:

- **Receive Jesus as your Prince of Peace.** If you have never experienced God's peace, admit your sin, turn from it, and turn to Jesus by faith. Then you will live in peace with God.

- **Enjoy true *shalom* in your relationship with God.** If you have received Christ as your Savior but are not experiencing wholeness, you may be stuck in a cycle of sin. Ask God to show you any areas of spiritual neglect and disobedience. Confess them, turn from them, and turn back to Him.

- **Live at peace with others.** Jesus our Peace has broken down all dividing walls. Is there a broken relationship in your life that needs to be made whole? Go to that person in the power of Christ and seek forgiveness and reconciliation.

*Challenge:* We live in a world full of chaos. Society tells us to work harder and do more. It can be easy to lose sight of this peace that is always available to us. Make a conscious effort this week to take a step back when tensions arise and call on *Jehovah Shalom*, God Our Peace.

*Pray:* Ask for prayer requests and ask group members to pray for the different requests as intercessors. As the leader, conclude by thanking God for being our Source of peace. Ask Him for the strength to share that message of peace with others this week.

# SESSION 5: OUR SHEPHERD

*The Point:* God guides us as He walks with us.

*The Passage:* Psalm 23:1-6

*The Setting:* Psalm 23 is attributed as "A Psalm of David." From his experiences as a shepherd when he was a young boy, David was able to take the imagery of shepherding and apply it to God as the Shepherd of his life. The psalm is a powerful testimony of David's trust in God's guidance and care in times of both peace and trial.

QUESTION 1: When has a guide made an experience more memorable?

> *Optional activity:* Display a few of the following items: a map, a compass, a cell phone with a navigational app, and handwritten directions. Ask: "In what scenario is each item most useful for directions? When is it least useful?" Explain that different scenarios call for different types of guidance. However, when it comes to navigating life, we have the ultimate guides: the Lord and the Holy Spirit.

*Video Summary:* This week we look at *Jehovah Rohi*—the Lord is Our Shepherd. The Bible often depicts us as sheep. Left to ourselves, we wander off and place ourselves in harm's way. The Bible also depicts God as the Shepherd over us. He is the One who gently guides us, protects us, and comforts us. Psalm 23 is one of the most beloved psalms in Scripture, and it succinctly captures this picture of God as our loving Shepherd.

▶ WATCH THE DVD SEGMENT FOR SESSION 5. THEN USE THE FOLLOWING QUESTIONS AND DISCUSSION POINTS TO TRANSITION INTO THE STUDY.

- What helps you stay close to the Shepherd in your daily life?
- How can you use Psalm 23 this week to share with someone else how God has been your Shepherd?

## WHAT DOES THE BIBLE SAY?

▶ ASK FOR A VOLUNTEER TO READ ALOUD PSALM 23:1-6.

Response: What's your initial reaction to these verses?

- What questions do you have about these verses?
- What new application do you hope to get from this passage?

▶ TURN THE GROUP'S ATTENTION TO PSALM 23:1-3.

QUESTION 2: In what ways have you experienced God's guidance in life?

Ask group members to keep things practical as they discuss this question. What specific practices have helped them distinguish God's guidance from other influences? As you discuss, encourage members to listen closely to the responses of others. Much can be learned in community.

> *Optional follow-up:* When have you felt like your soul was restored?

▶ MOVE TO PSALM 23:4-5.

**QUESTION 3:** When have you experienced God's presence in a dark valley?

The intent of this question is to move group members from Scripture interpretation to life application. In doing so, they will be better able to identify specific instances of God's presence in the midst of difficult times.

> ***Optional follow-up:*** When have you experienced your cup running over?

> ***Optional activity:*** Direct group members to complete the activity "God Our Shepherd" on page 43. As time permits, encourage volunteers to share their responses.

**QUESTION 4:** Which of the images in this passage is most meaningful to you right now?

This question requires group members to interpret the biblical text and then encourages them to consider what images most resonate with them in their current life circumstances. Encourage specific responses.

> ***Optional follow-up:*** How have you seen God's goodness and faithful love at work in your life?

▶ CONTINUE WITH PSALM 23:6.

**QUESTION 5:** How can our actions and attitudes demonstrate that we follow God as our Shepherd?

This is a question to be engaged and answered by your group as a whole. How can your group collectively communicate that they follow God as their Shepherd? Encourage them to be specific.

> ***Optional follow-up:*** How can your individual actions and attitudes demonstrate that you follow God as your Shepherd? Be specific.

**Note:** The following question does not appear in the Bible study book. Use it in your group discussion as time allows.

**QUESTION 6:** Psalm 23 clearly testifies to a faith tested by trials and a life mellowed and matured by the passing of years. In what ways have you experienced this in your own life?

Answering this question will give group members an opportunity to: (1) share from personal experience trials they have encountered in their lives; and (2) identify and process how God has worked in their lives through those trials and difficulties.

## LIVE IT OUT

How will a relationship with the Good Shepherd make a difference in your life? Encourage group members to choose one of the following applications:

- **Rest and trust.** When God doesn't provide what you think you need, trust His goodness. Spend some time this week thanking Him for His protection.

- **Stay close.** Sin will keep you from experiencing all the good the Shepherd desires for you. Acknowledge and confess any sin that keeps you separated from the One who desires to lead you to still waters.

- **Slow down.** If you are rushed and harried, it may be that you aren't taking time for the Shepherd to feed you and restore your soul. Make changes to your schedule to ensure more quality time in God's Word.

*Challenge:* We all need help with directions from time to time, whether we like to admit it or not. Thankfully we have the truest guide for life in *Jehovah Rohi*, God Our Shepherd. Watch for opportunities you may encounter this week to point others who are looking for direction to Him.

*Pray:* Ask for prayer requests and ask group members to pray for the different requests as intercessors. As the leader, conclude by thanking God for His guidance. Ask Him to help group members lead others to the one, true Guide in the coming week.

# SESSION 6: OUR RIGHTEOUSNESS

*The Point:* Because God is righteous, He will ultimately make all things right.

*The Passage:* Jeremiah 33:3-8,14-16

*The Setting:* The word of God came to Jeremiah in the last days of the kingdom of Judah. Because Jeremiah predicted the fall of Judah, neither he nor his prophecies were popular. Nor was his popularity helped by his call for the people to surrender to the invading Babylonians. Because of his prophesies, Jeremiah had been confined to the courtyard of the guard in the royal palace. But while God had given Jeremiah a message of judgment to proclaim to Judah, He gave Jeremiah a message of hope as well. God's judgment was not His final word against Judah. Judgment would be followed by hope and healing for the people of Judah and all of God's people.

QUESTION 1: As a kid, what made you say, "That's not fair!"?

> *Optional activity:* On a whiteboard or large sheet of paper, draw four squares and label them: right, wrong, right-wrong, and wrong-right. Ask group members to give examples of right things to do, wrong things to do, right things done for the wrong reasons, and wrong things done for the right reasons. Ask: "Which of these things pleases God?" Say: "Because God is righteous and we are not, we have a hard time with this if we don't look to Him for our standard."

*Video Summary:* The final video message of our study examines *Jehovah Tsidkenu*—God Our Righteousness. The text this week is Jeremiah 23 and 33. People with poor character, questionable ethics, and skewed morals seem to get ahead in life, while those who seek to do right seem to be passed by. In fact, people are often treated badly because of their right actions and character. We might be tempted to think God is unfair since He allows this to happen. But God is a righteous God. He will ultimately bring justice in all things.

▶ WATCH THE DVD SEGMENT FOR SESSION 6. THEN USE THE FOLLOWING QUESTIONS AND DISCUSSION POINTS TO TRANSITION INTO THE STUDY.

- What is your reaction to the statement, "Many non-Christians will judge our God based on our behavior."?
- What does it mean for us to represent a God who is righteous?

## WHAT DOES THE BIBLE SAY?

▶ ASK FOR A VOLUNTEER TO READ ALOUD JEREMIAH 33:3-8,14-16.

Response: What's your initial reaction to these verses?

- What questions do you have about how God makes all things right?
- What new application do you hope to get from this passage?

► TURN THE GROUP'S ATTENTION TO JEREMIAH 33:3-5.

QUESTION 2: What captures your attention about God's character in these verses?

Answers will vary as group members filter their responses through their own life experiences. This question provides an opportunity to interpret and internalize the biblical text as they share with the group.

*Optional follow-up:* When have you seen the benefits of discipline?

► MOVE TO JEREMIAH 33:6-8.

QUESTION 3: How have you experienced God's restoration?

This question provides group members with an opportunity to share a personal story based on their own life experiences.

*Optional follow-up:* In light of these verses, how would you explain God's grace?

► CONTINUE WITH JEREMIAH 33:14-16.

QUESTION 4: How do the promises in these verses point forward to Jesus?

This question asks group members to interpret the biblical text in terms of what can be learned about Jesus from this passage. Encourage them to look beyond the words.

*Optional follow-up:* What do you find hopeful in this passage? Why?

QUESTION 5: How can our actions and attitudes demonstrate that we follow God who is Our Righteousness?

This question is designed to help group members identify a personal call to action. Because this question is broad in scope, be prepared to start the discussion with some ideas of your own.

*Optional activity:* Direct group members to complete the activity "God Our Righteousness" on page 53. As time permits, encourage volunteers to share responses.

**Note:** The following question does not appear in the Bible study book. Use it in your group discussion as time allows.

QUESTION 6: How will God's promise of restoration affect the way you live your life?

This question provides group members with an opportunity to identify how biblical truth can positively impact the way they live their lives. Try to steer them away from talking theory; encourage them to be practical with their answers.

## LIVE IT OUT

God is Our Righteousness. How will you let that truth make a difference in your life? Invite group member to choose one of the following applications.

- **Confess.** Because God is righteous, He stands apart from sin. Enter into a relationship with Him, or restore your fellowship with Him, by confessing any sin in your life.

- **Trust.** Life is not always fair. Even when it feels like the wrong side is winning, God will have the final say. In the meantime, trust Him. He loves you, and in His righteousness, He will make things right.

- **Stand.** The trend in our culture is to believe we can each have our own definition of righteousness. Instead of becoming a standard to ourselves, Jesus is the standard for righteousness. Stand with Him and stand for Him in doing and proclaiming what is right.

*Challenge:* We all have plenty of examples of life not being fair. There are things in life we would like to see changed, but we have no control to change them. It's easy to become discouraged. But God is at work in positive ways in our lives and our world. That is why we can confidently approach Him. He knows our hearts and hears our concerns. Spend time talking to God this week. Allow Him to calm your heart. All will be made right in the end by *Jehovah Tsidkenu*, God Our Righteousness.

*Pray:* As the leader, close this final session of *God Is ...* in prayer. Thank God for the privilege of studying His Word throughout this resource. Conclude by thanking God for loving us and forgiving us. Ask Him for opportunities to share who He is with others this week.

**Note:** If you haven't discussed it yet, decide as a group whether or not you plan to continue to meet together and, if so, what Bible study options you would like to pursue. Visit LifeWay.com/smallgroups for help, or if you would like more studies like this one, visit biblestudiesforlife.com/smallgroups.

# Join the conversation

*Bible Studies for Life* is online!
There are lots of ways to interact with people around the world
who are going through the same Bible study as your group.

**facebook.com/biblestudiesforlife**
Interact with other group leaders and members. Ask questions.
Share stories. Get helpful links to additional resources.

**@biblemeetslife**
Follow us to stay up to date with our latest blog articles and other
*Bible Studies for Life* news. You can also respond to discussion
questions by using hashtags that go along with each session, such
as #BSFLpeace, or creating hashtags just for your group.

# My group's prayer requests